Calm & Colour
Floral

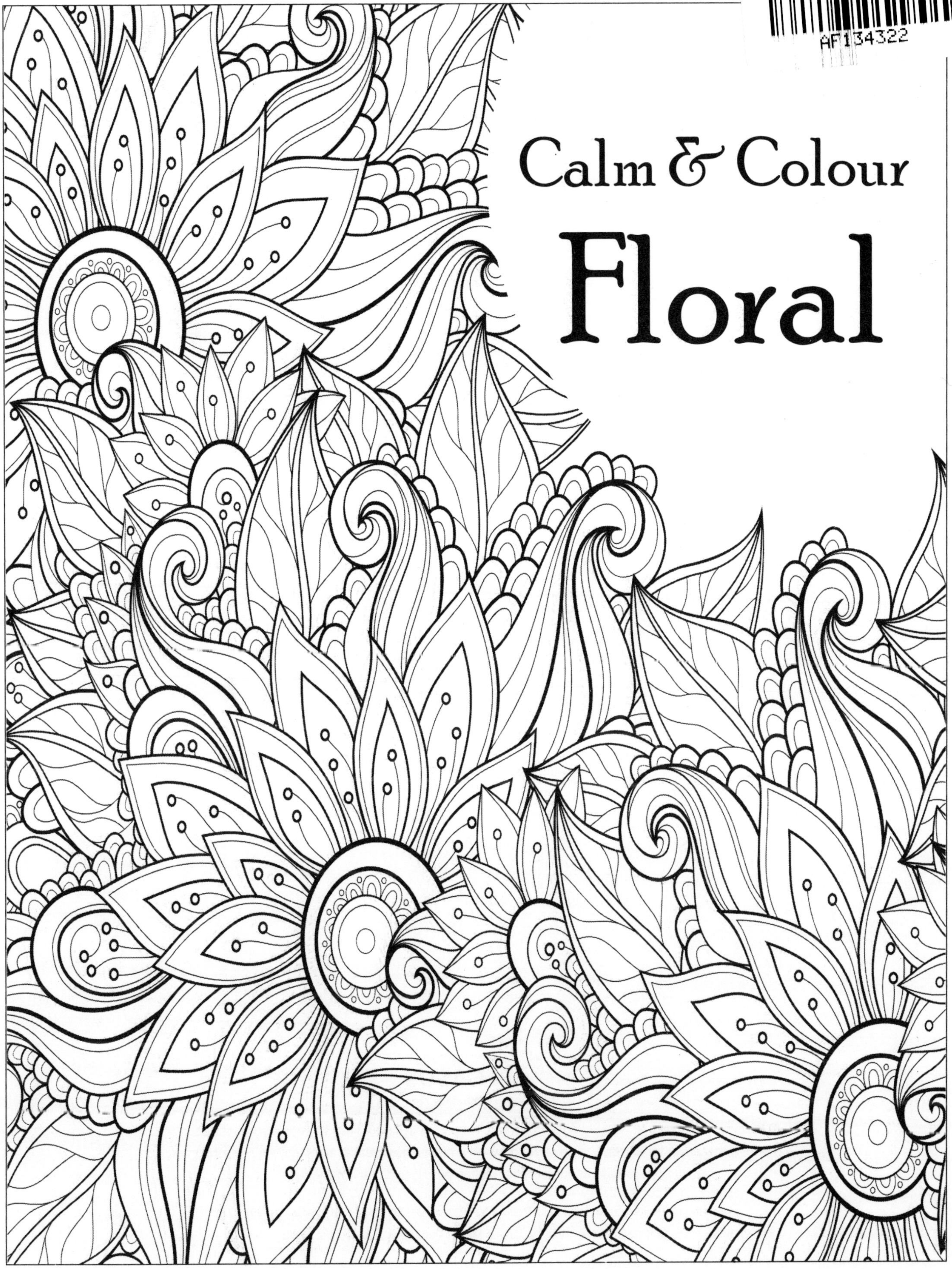

PEGASUS

www.pegasusforkids.com

Published by Kuldeep Jain for B. Jain Publishers (P) Ltd., D-157, Sector 63, Noida - 201307, U.P

Registered office: 1921/10, Chuna Mandi, Paharganj, New Delhi-110055

Printed in India

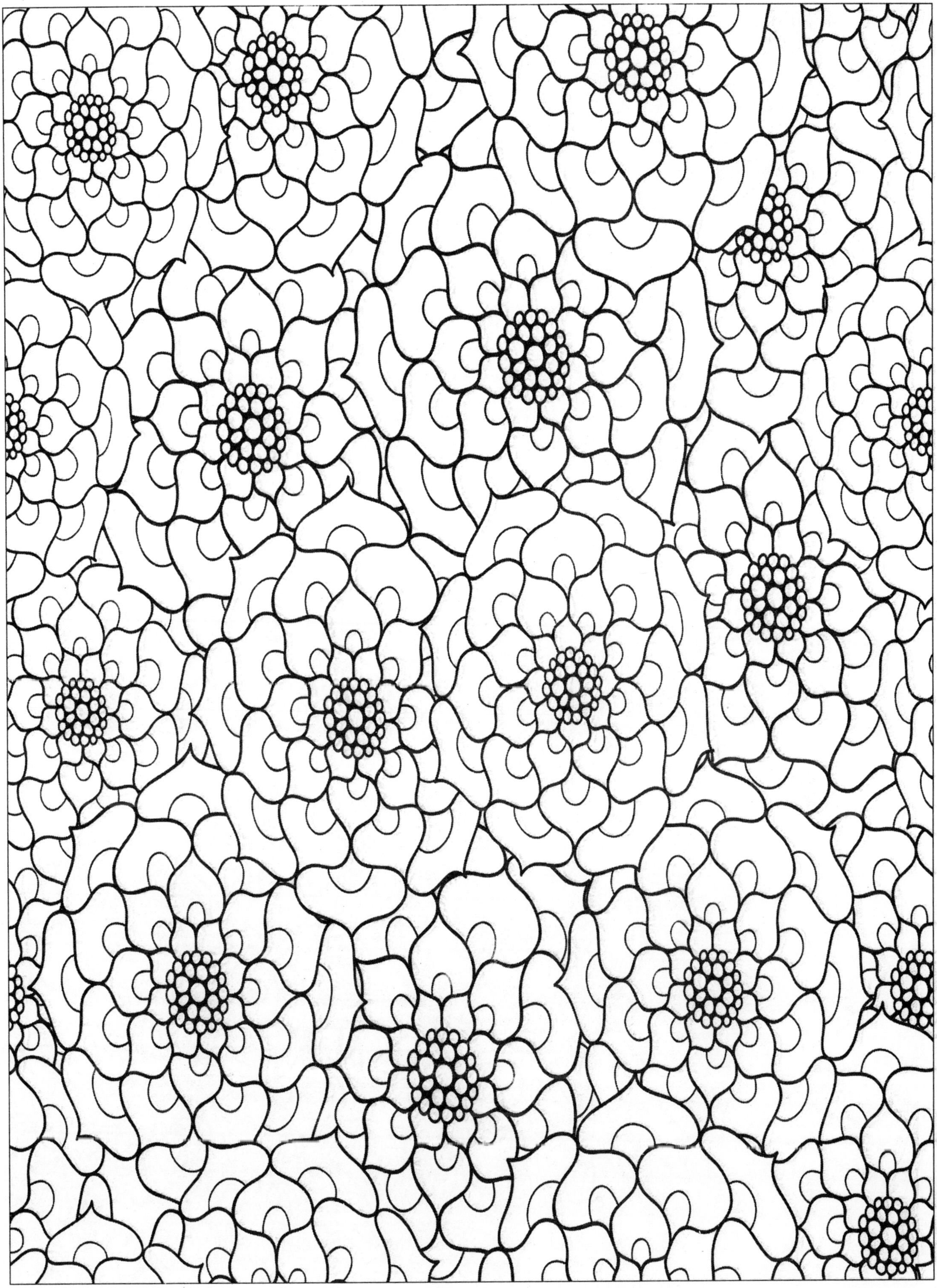